We are all Adrift

Text, Images - David Banning
Drawings - Iain Sharpe

Introduction by Philip Hoare

CHROMA EDITIONS

We are all Adrift

Text, Images & Design by David Banning

Drawings by Iain Sharpe

Introduction by Philip Hoare

First published in the United Kingdom in 2025 by
Chroma Editions
38 Brendjean Road
Morecambe
Lancashire
LA4 5SE

www.chromaeditions.com

ISBN: 978-1-8380915-7-6

HARBOUR (Noun)
A place on the coast where ships may moor in shelter, especially one protected from rough water by piers, jetties and other artificial structures.

(Verb)
To hide and protect
To keep feelings or thoughts
To contain and allow development

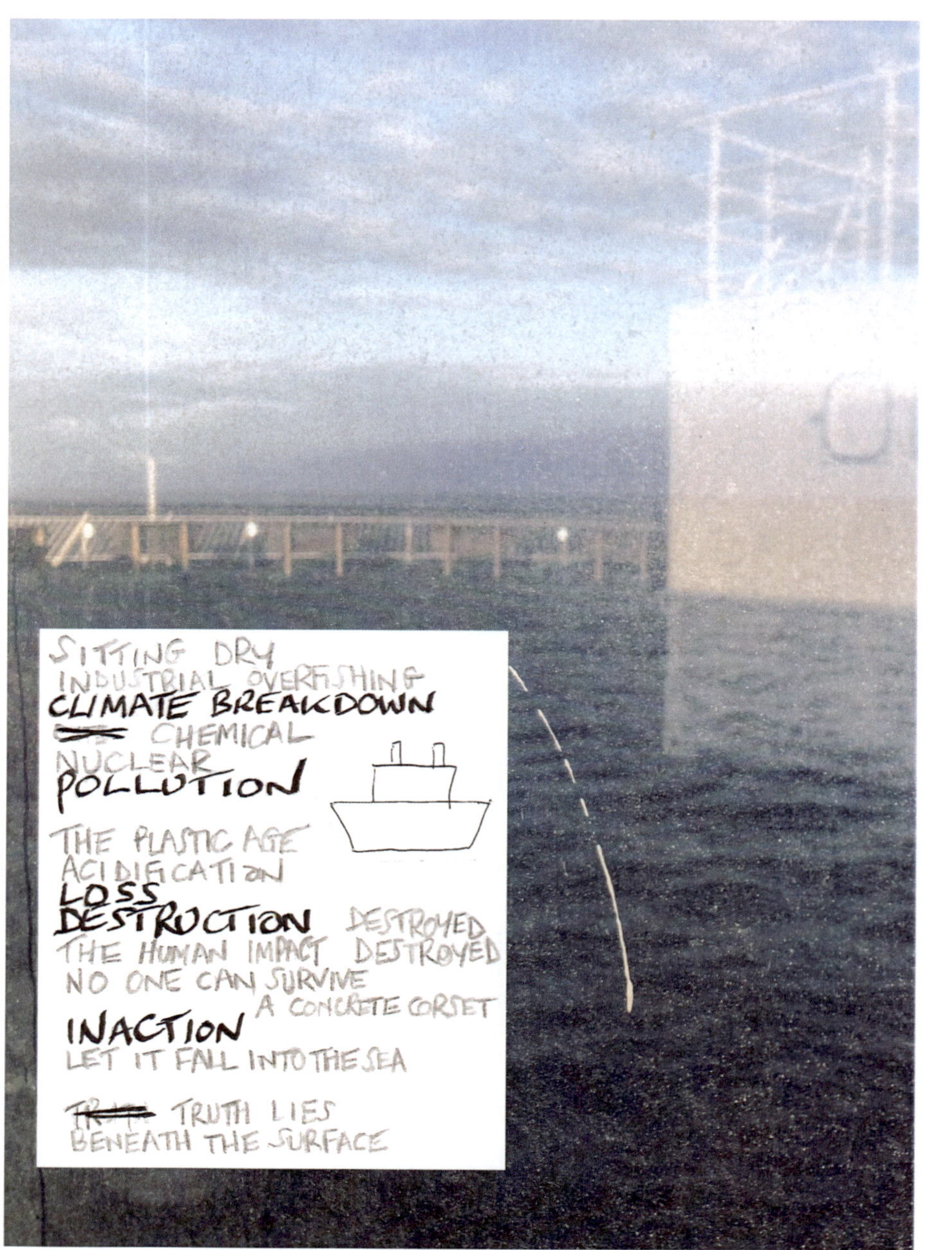
SITTING DRY
INDUSTRIAL OVERFISHING
CLIMATE BREAKDOWN
CHEMICAL
NUCLEAR
POLLUTION
THE PLASTIC AGE
ACIDIFICATION
LOSS
DESTRUCTION DESTROYED
THE HUMAN IMPACT DESTROYED
NO ONE CAN SURVIVE
A CONCRETE CORSET
INACTION
LET IT FALL INTO THE SEA
TRUTH LIES
BENEATH THE SURFACE

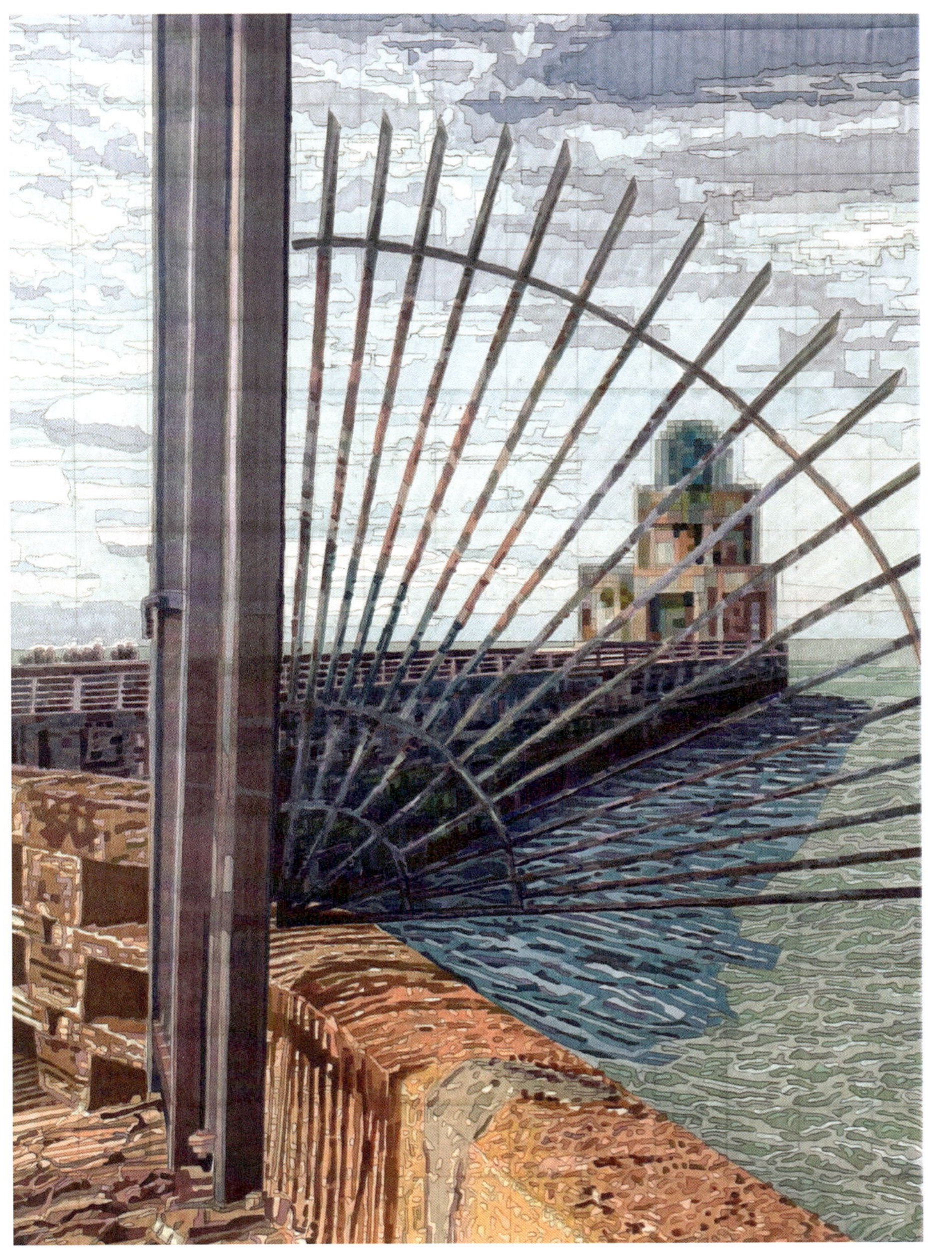

fig.1

Stations of Encounter

Where
do we go?
into a
promised utopia
where boundaries
shift and change
mobility across
oceans a shadow
army of foreign
faces divided
against itself
mistaken souls
waiting hopelessly
at the border
gateways the
channel surrounds
yet no water
can be found
in the long
silence of
conflict
and
loss

There is no country for those who despair, but I know that the sea comes before and after me, and hold my madness ready. Each wave brings its promise, always the same. What does the wave say?
(Albert Camus - *The Sea Close By*)

They say the immigrants steal the hubcaps of respected gentlemen.
They say it would be wine and roses if England were for Englishmen again.
(The Clash - *Something About England*)

Nothing is more precious than independence and liberty…
(attributed to Ho Chi Minh)

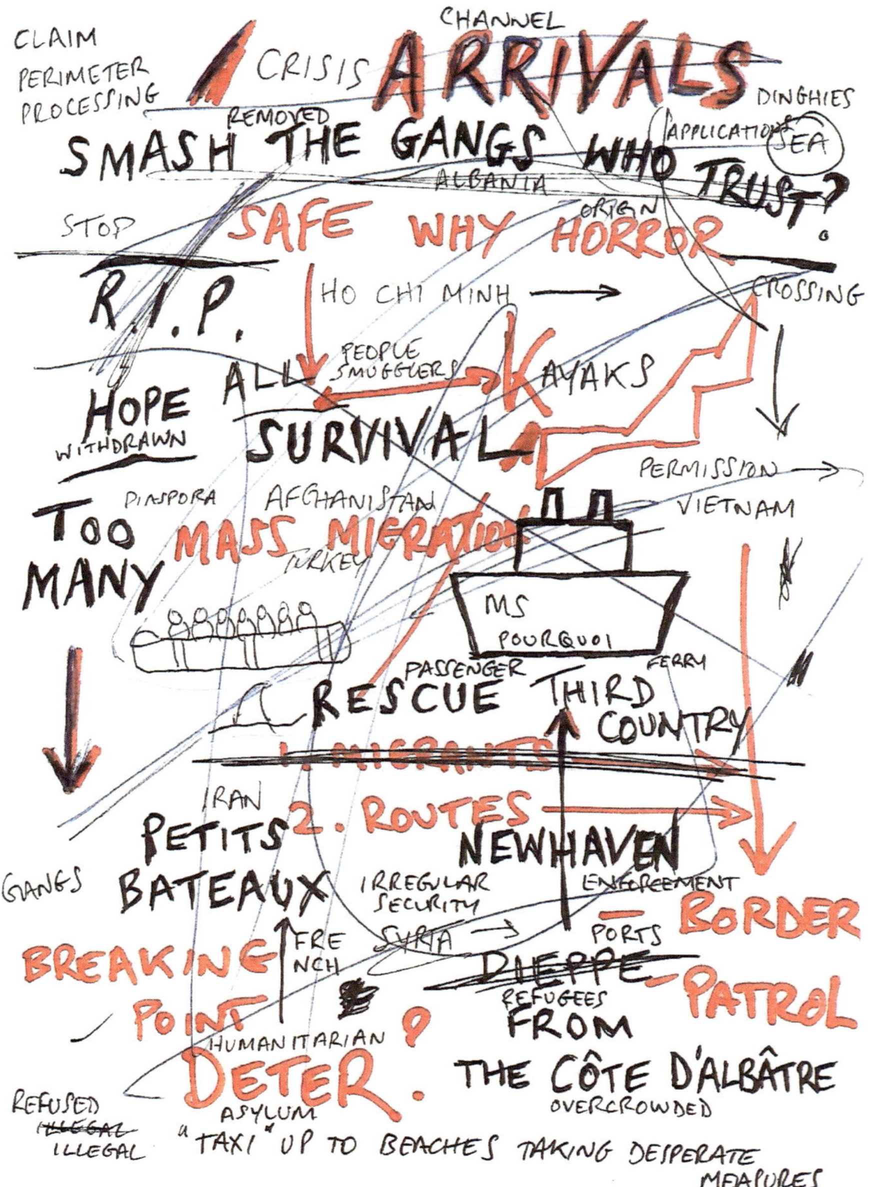
CLAIM
PERIMETER
PROCESSING
CRISIS
CHANNEL
ARRIVALS
DINGHIES
REMOVED
SMASH THE GANGS
WHO TRUST?
APPLICATIONS
SEA
ALBANIA
STOP
SAFE
WHY
ORIGIN
HORROR
R.I.P.
HO CHI MINH
CROSSING
PEOPLE
SMUGGLERS
KAYAKS
HOPE
ALL
SURVIVAL
WITHDRAWN
PERMISSION
DIASPORA
AFGHANISTAN
VIETNAM
TOO
MANY
MASS MIGRATION
TURKEY
MS
POURQUOI
PASSENGER
FERRY
RESCUE
THIRD
COUNTRY
1. MIGRANTS
IRAN
2. ROUTES
PETITS
BATEAUX
NEWHAVEN
GANGS
IRREGULAR
SECURITY
ENFORCEMENT
BORDER
SYRIA
PORTS
BREAKING
POINT
FRENCH
DIEPPE
REFUGEES
FROM
PATROL
HUMANITARIAN
DETER.
THE CÔTE D'ALBÂTRE
REFUSED
ILLEGAL
ILLEGAL
ASYLUM
OVERCROWDED
"TAXI" UP TO BEACHES
TAKING DESPERATE
MEASURES

Introduction by Philip Hoare

The sea and memory are intimately related, fluid, elusive, encompassing. Coming and going, more dreams than you can take. History, evolution, terror, despair, mortality and beauty begin there. Human and non-human, forever connected by it, since that's where we all came from.

We harbour jealousy and fear, longing and desire. The sea is where laws run out. A new jurisdiction takes over there. It puts its arms around us. Art and language draw us in, too. David Banning's publication leaves us knowing just a little bit more about all of this.

That's all you could ask for, isn't it?

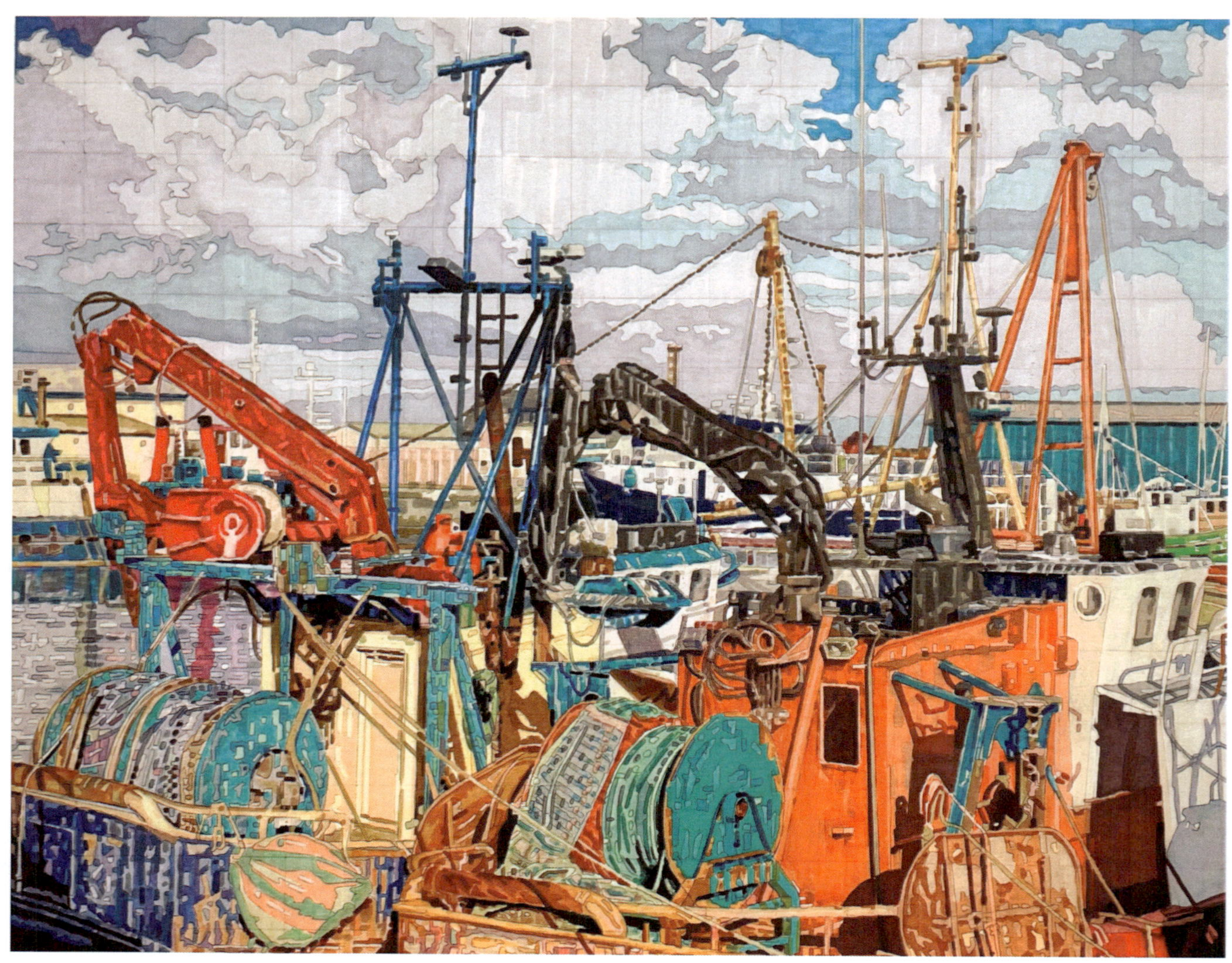

fig.2

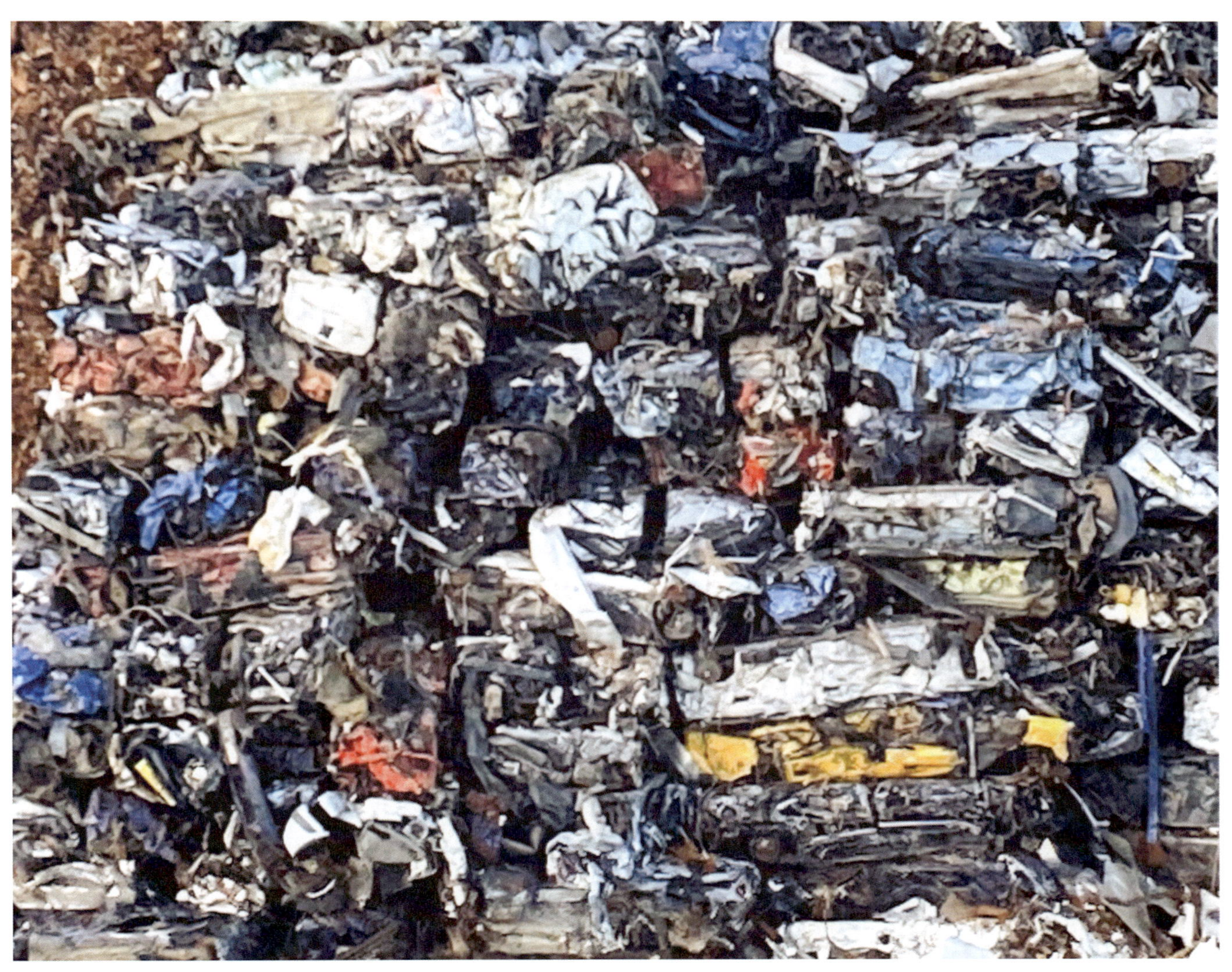

fig.3

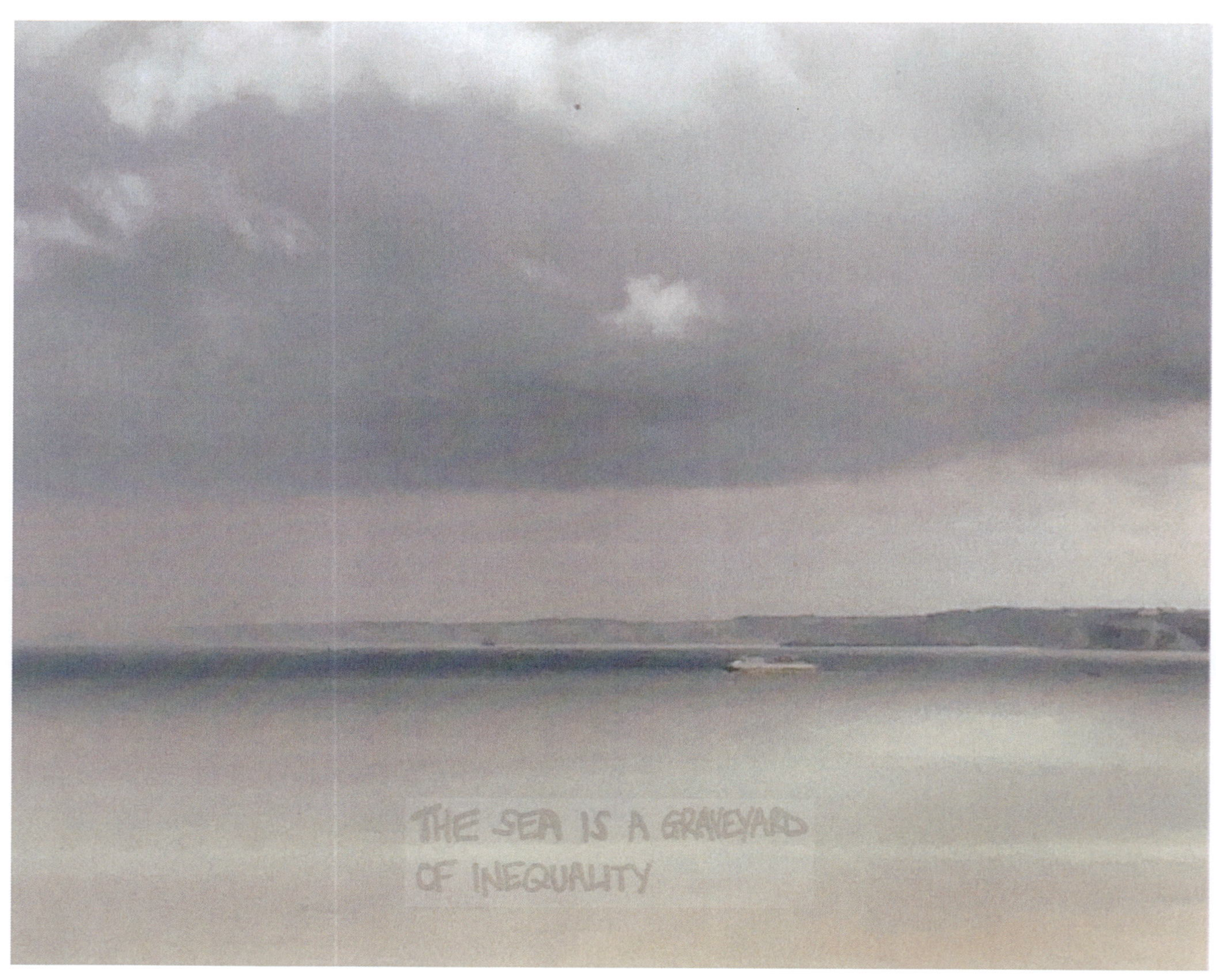
THE SEA IS A GRAVEYARD
OF INEQUALITY

We are all Adrift

Logbook

Low tide, mid-February…
In the melancholy hour the ebbing sun dissolves anxieties into misty air. Unfolding its wings, darkness begins to settle on the West Quay of Newhaven harbour. Glancing at the water's edge, I stretch out my arms and gently tilt my head forwards and backwards for a few seconds. A lengthy journey from Lancashire included its usual patchwork of roadworks, lane closures and temporary speed zones. The familiar 320 mile slog from the intertidal mudflats of Morecambe Bay to the mouth of the River Ouse never fails. Where the sea meets the South Downs on the south coast, the two towns may be connected by proud maritime origins, but they still smoulder from the effects of late twentieth century decline. 'Trust me to live so far away' I thought, my mother being in a care home on the outskirts of Eastbourne roughly 10 miles away. To meet the considerable monthly fees we took the inevitable heartbreaking decision of selling her home in the midst of Covid. I've been visiting her now for over four years. She seems happier there most of the time. Now, as I look back, I begin to realise how my visits to Newhaven have marked the beginning of an erasure that has fragmented my life ever since.

In the rise and fall of the English Channel familiar patterns are bound with layers of messages and meanings that would otherwise have remained hidden. The harbour's mystery and transience always seems to evoke places where I have lived before. A point of thinness transcends an enormous psychedelic ocean of space and time that stops at a point where there is nothing but grey seawater, mudflats and emptiness. Once or twice a year, I combine visits to Newhaven with the short hop over to Normandy on the Dieppe ferry. Suffocating in the Tory government's false euphoria post-Brexit, I sensed an opportunity to shed light on the mental blockage between the former co-imperialists. Too often this is a mendacious narrative wrapped up in the transitory process of decolonisation that began with the American War of Independence against Britain (1776), and continued through the fallout of the First World War, Britain's involvement in the partitions of India and Palestine until the culmination in the 1950s of France's defeats in Indo-China, Tunisia, Morocco and the Algerian War of Independence.

C'était pour toujours…

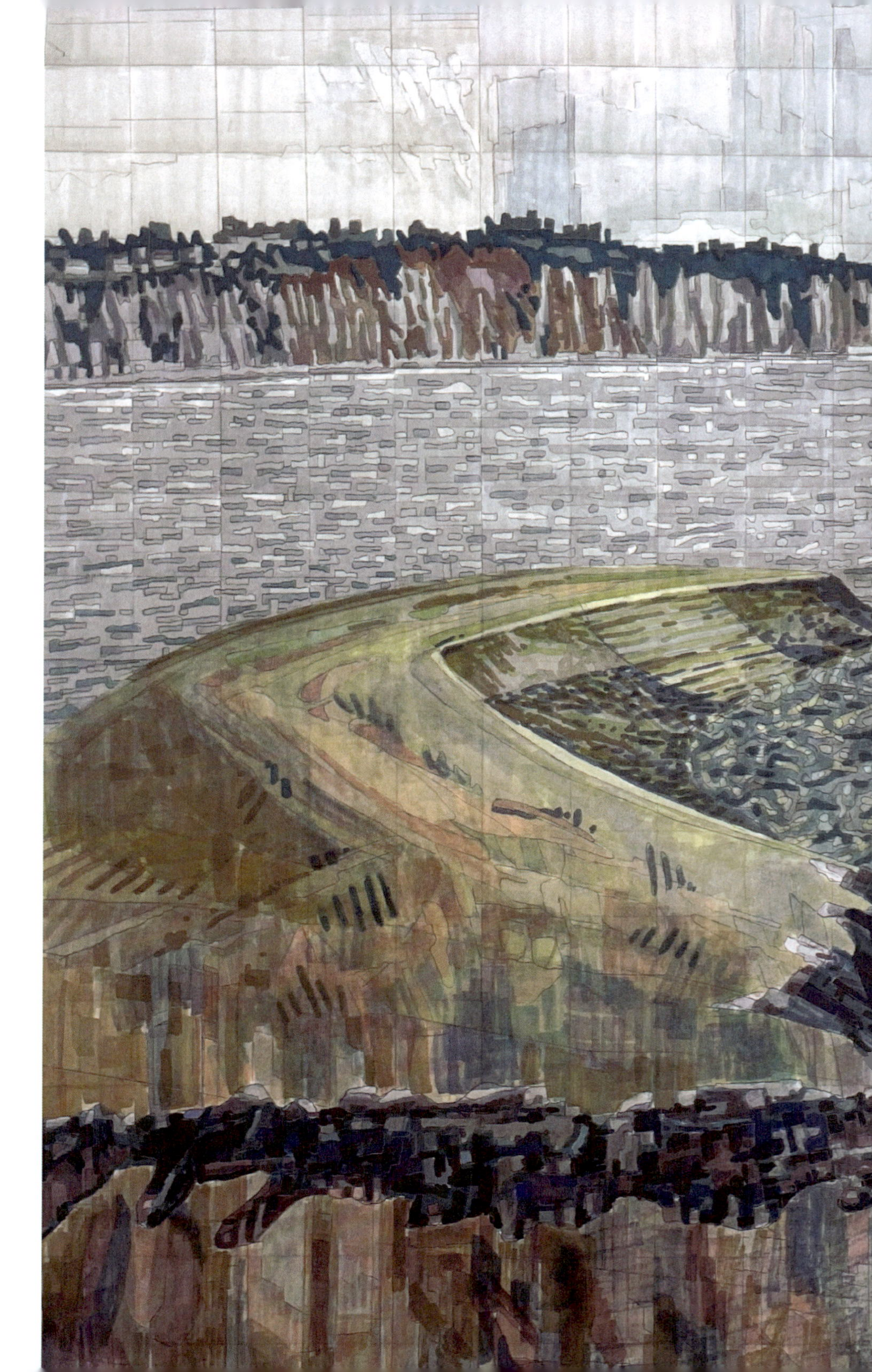

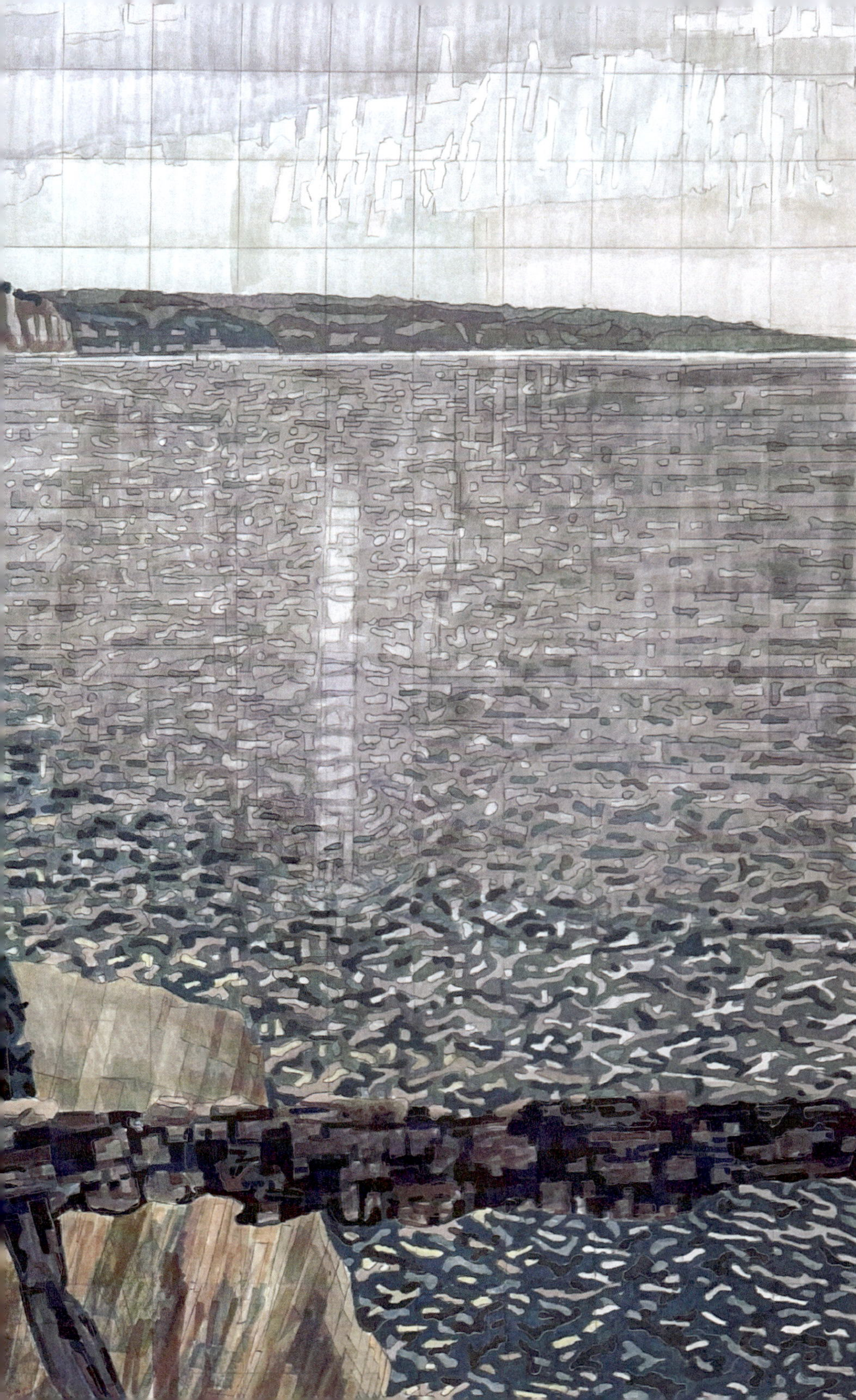

fig.4

Ideas, combinations and interpretations – according to the Institut Culinaire De France, “to be a successful pastry chef you have to be aware of everything around you so that you can draw inspiration from it”. In the years leading up to the First World War, you could imagine the revolutionary politician, Ho Chi Minh peering into a murky future when he worked as a pastry chef on the cross-channel ferry service between Newhaven and Dieppe. Based in London and Paris, he travelled widely on French ships before visiting the Soviet Union in 1923. Known by his real name, Nguyen Sinh Cung he began training at Moscow’s *Comintern*, an organisation created by Lenin to encourage worldwide revolution. After spending the 1930s roaming and campaigning in Russia and China, he returned to Vietnam to lead the struggle for independence from Japanese and French colonial rule. While founding the communist-controlled independence movement, Viet Minh, he changed his name to Ho Chi Minh - the ‘Bringer of Light’. Battle lines remained drawn for another three decades until the 1950s. In modern times, a small token of this considerable legacy includes a foundation stone marking the 100th anniversary of his arrival in the UK (1913-2013).

I sit on one of four triangular shaped blocks of concrete blackened by mud surrounding Ho Chi Minh's stone. Spinning in the dark, waves slosh from side to side before curling round the timber stilts perched over the seawater. Behind me on the cobblestones, a discarded pallet bleached by salt water, wind and sun matches the shiftless pallor of cloud ridden skies. At first the monument divided a town hollowed out by shattering austerity cuts to public services. The erasure of the High Street advanced so rapidly that Newhaven began to resemble a no man's land with the closure of banks, supermarkets and other retail outlets. Despite growing unease, the council held firm, citing the combined benefit of culture, education, economy and tourism. Reports in the local media suggested a number of constituent's letters and emails refused to believe that Ho Chi Minh's stone would provide a 'suitable' role model for Newhaven. Thankfully, the so-called 'dead town' received a much needed boost in 2017 with the arrival of an Enterprise Zone, set up to encourage new businesses into the area. One of its major aims was to entice ferry passengers to "park up and spend money in the town" rather than speed off to join the millions heading to more fashionable tourist destinations. Brighton, its large and diverse big brother (often referred to as one of the UK's most hip cities) lies in wait just ten miles up the South Coast Road. Almost a decade on however, Newhaven's business incentives appear to be bearing fruit with new cafes, restaurants and even an art trail providing sparkly showers of hope.

I wanted to stay next to the stone, but a sense of gloom began eating into the moonless night. With the cold seeping through me I knew it would be foolish to linger there for much longer. Gliding by overhead the yelping cries of gulls contrasted perfectly with the chirping melodies of sparrows and blackbirds busying themselves in the shrubs and trees of a nearby recreation ground. There was hardly anyone else about, save for a few nighthawks gazing out from the Falaise flat complex overlooking the harbour.

The freedom of modern life breeds Hopperesque souls, all alone yet all together, shielded by cold plate glass windows next to the lifeboat station. The harbour must protect and hold everyone intact. Scanning back towards the electric swing bridge, I noticed that the names of a couple of fishing boats contained the word 'Meeching'. A word derived from the Anglo Saxon 'Meces' meaning 'the people of the camp of the sword'. Researching online I discovered that the Saxons arrived in 477AD, following the Roman withdrawal from Britain. On the banks of the Ouse below Castle Hill they founded a village called Meeching. In the Middle Ages the mouth of the river was located eastwards toward Seaford, until a momentous storm in 1579 blocked the area and breached the river at an expanse of shingle further west between Meeching and Seaford. The resulting flood straightened the southern section of the river and the cutting created a harbour entrance – New Haven. Relics such as Stone Age flints, Neolithic pottery and Bronze and Iron Age items have been found at Castle Hill, where the view from the ramparts offers a splendid 360: the harbour to the Ouse Estuary, the Downs, Seaford Head and out across the English Channel. Next to Castle Hill, a Nature Reserve contained a variety of flora and fauna that thrives in the chalk downland of the South Downs National Park.

IMAGINARY PEOPLE
SWELLING FROM THE DEPTHS
~~HISTORICAL AMNESIA~~
ABSORBED IN THE OCEAN BED
IN RISING WATER LEVELS
THAT SUBMERGE AND DISRUPT
FIRING FLARES OF HOSTILITY
ENVELOPED IN SMOKE AND FLAME
TERROR AND HORROR WILL FALL
AS BLOOD FLOWS IN THE CHANNEL
FLOATING IN DIRTY WATER
A MELANGE OF THE UNWASHED
"~~WHY ARE WE HERE?~~"

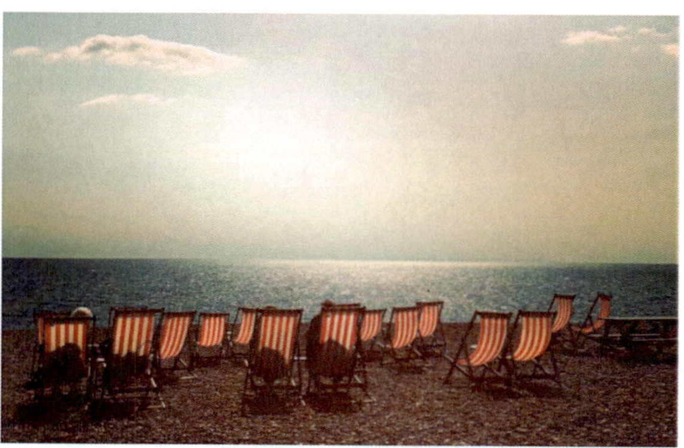

HAHAHAHA
STOP
THE
BOATS
LOL....

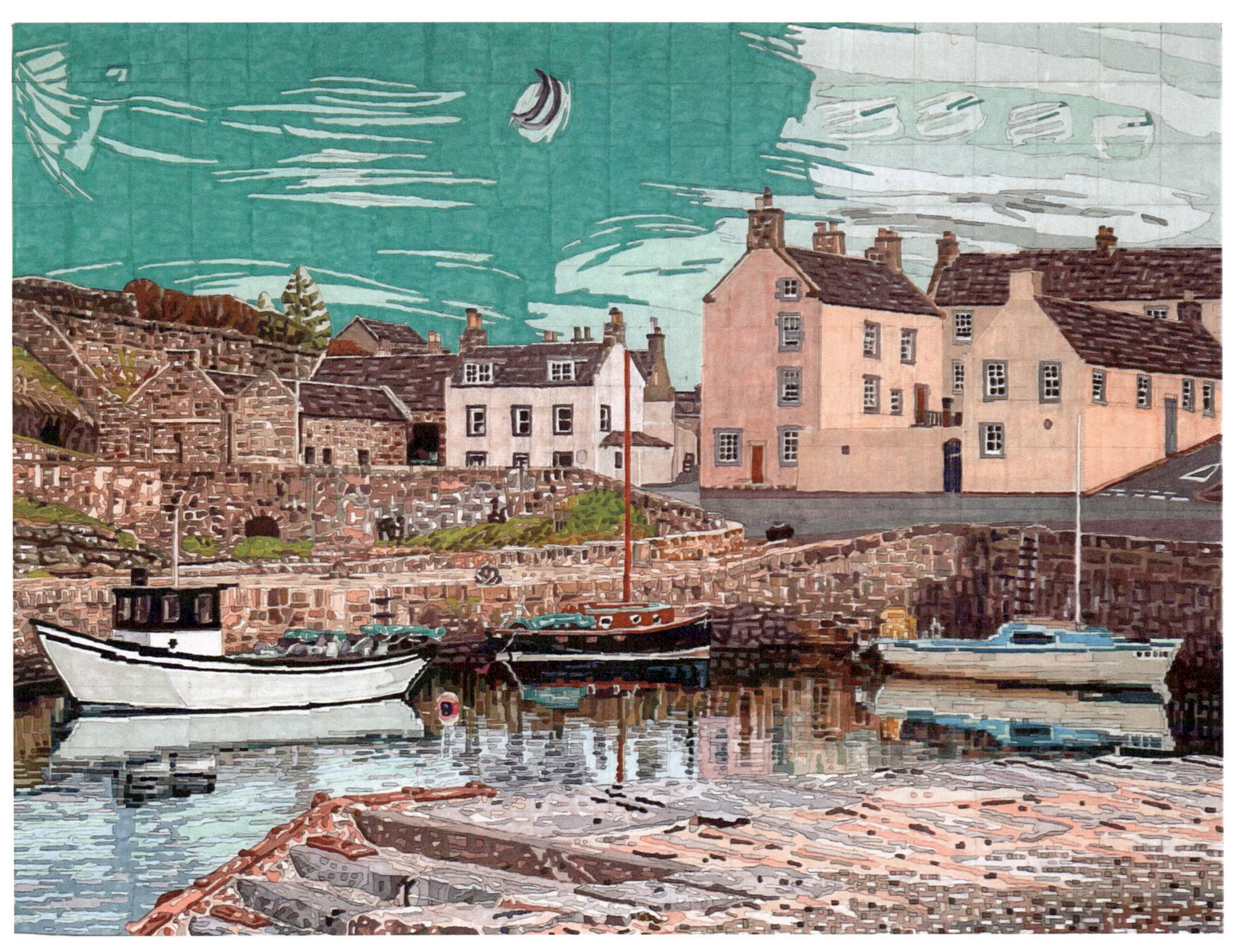

fig.5

In a post truth world, rising water levels are mapped into micro-conflict zones of resistance, abandonment and freedom. Floating in dirty water, waves of unwashed bodies tremble like silent oblivions beached upon the shore. Slow deaths or new beginnings. From Castle Hill's commanding viewpoint (another Site of Special Scientific Interest), the coastguard keeps an eye out for sinister cargo. Constructed out of an impressive 6 million bricks, Newhaven Fort marks the spot where the Victorians built the largest work of defence ever constructed in Sussex. Fearing a French invasion, Lord Palmerston commissioned the fortress in the 1860s to protect the harbour entrance. Designated as a Scheduled Ancient Monument, the stronghold underwent considerable updating throughout both World

Slow deaths or new beginnings

Wars including the construction of gun emplacements during the World War II. Fear and loathing in the modern era repeats similar patterns of hostility. A terrible past that waits hopelessly at the gates of Europe with borders, loopholes, quotas and foreigners absorbed in the bed of the English Channel. Welcome to the media's 'Tinderbox Britain', where the liberal establishment vision of a modern multicultural Britain simmers like a frayed temper in a heatwave. The reawakening of raw working class pride stoked by opportunist far-right activists appears to be something straight out of the late 1970s playbook. Remember Notting Hill, Southall and The Battle of Lewisham? In 2024, anger spilled out and rippled across the North-West of England after horrific stabbings at a Taylor

Slow deaths or new beginnings

Swift dance class in Southport. Rioters even attempted to set fire to a hotel housing migrants in Rotherham French newspaper Libération ran the headline a 'Disunited Kingdom'. Force fed a seductive diet of divisive rumours the civil war was supposed to have been started by racists, terrorists, and left behind out-of-towners who joined ranks to vent their anger on the streets. A few press reports claimed the majority of disorder was caused by people who lived within a 5-mile radius of the disturbances. A year on, fresh calls go out from online networks, encouraging people to converge on fortified hotels housing asylum seekers banned from working. Under red, white and blue banner text, slogans on social media stir up rebellion, 'Protect Our Community, Safety of Women and Chil dren before Foreigners, All Patriots Welcome". In globalism's fractured mess an old ism has re-emerged. *Patriotism* - Gen Z's defiant battle cry - are you taking orders or are you taking over? The crazed mysticism of flags…We want our country back…while the so-called 'great dividers' lament the 'dilution of Englishness' rollers continue to break in the long, even lines along Normandy beaches. The historic D-Day beaches once surrounded by pre-fabricated harbours providing access for Allied troops entering Europe are once again points of departure in a new lethal trade of human hope. Another 'Great Crusade' in the choppy waters of the English Channel where discarded life-jackets, rucksacks and petrol canisters litter the scrublands of Northern France. Successive governments

We want our country back

can find no quick fix to a fresh Orwellian future fuelled by hostility and a deeply felt sense of difference. Once again the old dictum resurfaces sending sombre shivers of despair, 'imagine a boot stamping on a human face – forever'. *Envoyez-les chez eux…*

Rising from the murky depths, the heady scent of rotting seaweed hangs like a mixture of bad eggs and halitosis. A progressively more common toxic invader that has flourished in recent years due to warming oceans, high winds, sewage discharge and agricultural run-off. Sometimes the stench of these blooms can spread over whole towns for days without end. I took a few steps back from the surging foam and smiled at someone draping a dark blue cover over a luxury speedboat intriguingly

We want our country back

named 'Lady Maverick'. *Be Unorthodox. Be a Free Spirit. Be a Maverick.* Book your adventure today! Maverick Boat Adventures from Newhaven to the iconic Seven Sisters Cliffs. Tasting the unique experience of whizz and fizz on the waves, whoopin' and a hollerin' to sound system bangers. Except tomorrow's thrills might have to be postponed given several failed attempts to start the engine. As dusk fell, strong gusts buffeted the buoys and sails producing an eerie clanking that stretched and expanded throughout the marina and beyond. Like a torrent of church bells grieving all at once. *Si seulement j'avais un bateau* …As the metallic rotations reverberated, over on the East Quay cutting through the jingle-jangle symphony, the mammoth structure of a suction hopper dredger appeared

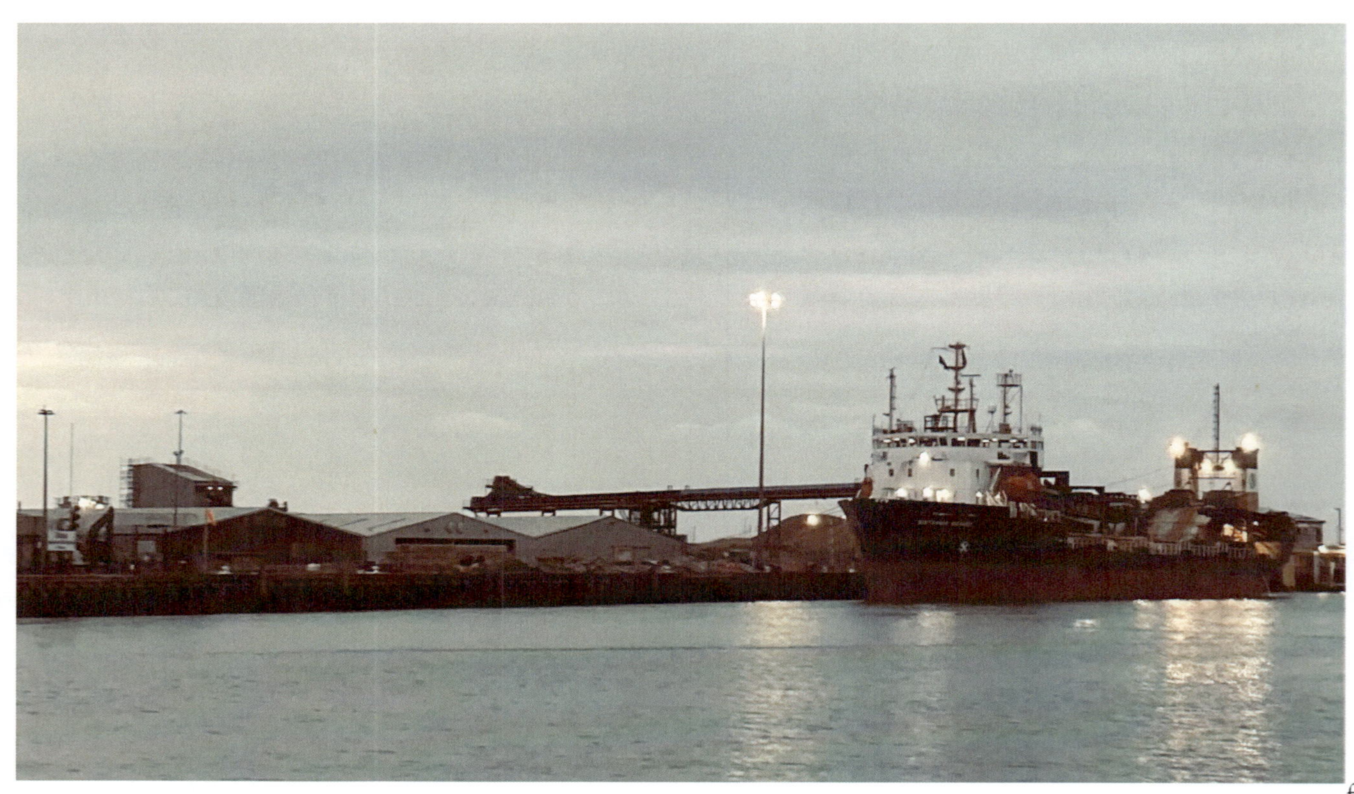

fig.6

shrouded by mist. Dredging the depths for aggregates, the £12 million 'A' class 'Britannia Beaver' (custom built in Devon) has been operational since 1992. Working almost all year round, it is capable of combing the seabed to depths of 45 metres. Delivering sand and gravel to wharves in the South East of England and other countries in the EU, it also has access to sand and gravel deposits in the North Sea and English Channel close to the Isle of Wight. Dredging of the harbour is a necessary occurrence enhancing infrastructure and supporting local construction efforts. In January 2024, the Britannia Beaver helped to donate 20 tonnes of marine dredged aggregates to Newhaven FC, enabling the football club to create a new car park in an area of open ground prone to flooding.

On previous visits, I often used to wonder why a towering scrapheap on the East Quay had been allowed to cast a lingering spell on the quayside for so long. Such an ostentatious pile with matching stench, some first impression for ferry passengers from France – *Bienvenue Mesdames et Messieurs*…However, to the relief of long suffering residents and visitors, the eyesore has completely vanished. Apparently, H. Ripley's monstrosity was finally quietly relocated 'somewhere' along the River Thames. Seized by the authorities the swamp of rejects moves on to fight another day. Another recent development has seen the approval of the third phase of the West Quay Regeneration Project masterminded by Morgan Carn Architects. Unanimously agreed by Lewes District Council's planning committee in 2024, a substantial regeneration package is hoped to be the catalyst for further investment. Joining the ranks of reimagined shoes, laptops, teabags and cars, the marina's new vision incorporates 400 riverside homes, a 50 bedroom apartment hotel with gym, various restaurants and cafes with the 300 berth marina reconfigured with greatly improved facilities. In amongst all the grandiose waffle, there are plans for the continuation of the Riverside Walkway allowing public access to the waterfront. My attention drifted to a flashing green light near the harbour entrance. As I turned to head back toward the direction of the Scuba Diving Centre, I nodded at an elderly fisherman covered with rags carrying an assortment of ropes, reels and buckets. Stopping briefly outside the Fort Road café, I cupped an ear toward the distant rumble of commuters on the A27. Slicing through the heart of Ravilious country, for some, the artist's watercolours and illustrations evoke a timeless period that harks back to Ancient Britain. Especially since the chalky downlands have mostly escaped the greedy claws of modernity's ongoing expansion. Like the sea, the landscape of the South Downs is shaped and formed in the imagination, infused with a sense of idealised nostalgia hiding greater truths. Although born in Acton (West London) at the turn of the twentieth century, Eric Ravilious grew up in Eastbourne. The name Ravilious is derived from the French (possibly in some corrupted form after a Huguenot refugee) from names like Revel, Revelion, Revalier, Rivalin and Revelliod. From the early 1930s, he made a significant contribution to the development of English Neo Romantic landscape art. During this period his work also developed an enduring connection between Morecambe and Newhaven. In 1933, architect Oliver Hill had been overseeing the construction of a new Midland Railway Hotel to compliment the curve of Morecambe's promenade.

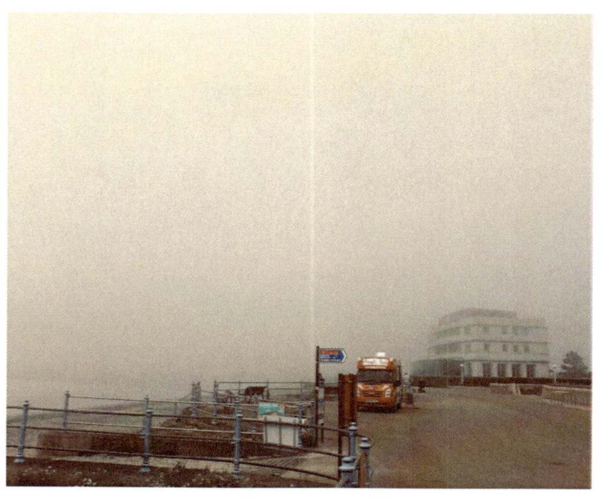

With the aim of attracting tourists from the Lake District into the town, construction progressed at such a quick pace that an opening date of July 12th had already been fixed. Hill commissioned Ravilious to design and execute a mural for the circular tea room and bar along with his namesake the controversial sculptor, typesetter and engraver Eric Gill who had been asked to create a piece for the dining room.

Gill and Ravilious knew other from producing illustrations for the Golden Cockerel Press, but Gill's crimes (uncovered in personal journals after his death) would change the way the world saw him. There can be no unknowing an extraordinary artist who will forever challenge the notion of whether art and life can ever be separated. Ravilious and his artist wife Tirzah Garwood worked on decorating the tea room and bar immediately after they arrived in early April. They soon ran into major problems due to the general conditions of the inside of the building. Floods to the roof, a dripping wet ceiling and peeling walls are all mentioned in the diary Tirzah kept at the time. She voices continual concerns that their daytime and night time seaside scenes would not 'take' properly. Even though the plaster had not completely dried out the hotel completion date would not be moved back. Inevitably, after it opened, cracks soon began to appear in several places necessitating a programme of constant patching up. They tried repairing the artwork one last time, returning to what Tirzah referred to as the 'big white concrete ship' the following March. Despite carrying out extensive repairs, Eric and Tirzah's mural quickly deteriorated again, suffering the final ignominy of being painted over. It would not be seen again until the late 1980s when set designers for Thames Television had the idea to reproduce the mural in its original location while filming an episode for the TV detective series '*Agatha Christie's Poirot*.' An enduring tribute to the original murals was painted in situ almost eighty years later in 2013, by the artist Jonquil Cook and her assistant Isa Clee-Cadman. Not long after their travails at the Midland, Ravilious produced two striking works of Newhaven harbour.

At the beginning of August 1936, he arrived in Newhaven to spend a week of intensive painting with fellow artist Edward Bawden. While he walked the length of the jetty to look at the lighthouse a tremendous storm blew up, prompting comparisons with Turner who allegedly tied himself to the mast of a ship heading into a weighty storm. Ravilious chose Newhaven Harbour as the subject for a colour lithograph produced by a newly formed company called Contemporary Lithographs. The stunning luminosity of the uninhabited scene he depicted certainly does not in any way evoke the danger and fear of a storm. In fact his own title for the painting was, '*Homage to Seurat*', the French post-impressionist painter best known for the painting technique of Pointillism. Featuring a boat leaving the harbour, the other work, a watercolour *Channel Steamer* was selected by the Tate Gallery for exhibition at the 1939 World's Fair in New York.

The strangeness of life has always preoccupied me…The unknowingness

Collecting and exhibiting contemporary art for over 100 years, the Towner Art Gallery, Eastbourne has become another place of refuge during my brief sojourns in East Sussex. Twinned with the cult of Ravilious, they have a dedicated space housing a special display of his works running alongside a vigorous programme of contemporary exhibitions. Despite Ravilious' rightful reputation as one of Sussex's most celebrated artists, it is the work of another painter with strong associations to Towner to whom I have been most drawn. Harold Mockford notably described himself as a 'provincial artist' when comparing himself with the more 'avant garde' abstract painters of his generation. Born in 1932, he lived in Eastbourne and Newhaven for most of his life, producing accomplished works of art from the age of fifteen. Ultimately, Mockford gained a deserved reputation as a fine lyrical artist whose distinctive paintings will be remembered for the deep colours of their land, sea, and townscapes. As a boy, he was evacuated several times during the Second World War, but still managed to spend most of his youth out on the South Downs. Recognising an early talent for drawing, one of his teachers persuaded him to attend Saturday morning art classes at The Towner. He left school to become an apprentice dental technician before meeting his future wife Margaret Beney at a local youth club. Mainly self-taught, Mockford attended evening life drawing classes while working full-time and raising a family with Margaret.

After joining the Eastbourne Group of Artists, he produced a formidable body of work between 1959 and 2012, exhibiting in London and across south-east England. Typically using oil on board, his work is held in various collections including Tate Britain, Towner, and the Government Art Collection. In 1958, William Gear, the newly appointed curator at Towner (an abstract painter himself), purchased the gallery's first Mockford, simply titled *Eastbourne.* The painting triggered outrage among the local community who considered it a waste of money and misrepresentation of the town. Ironically, it was the first of his oils that I encountered at Towner, and still my favourite. Viewed from above like a premonition of Google Earth's seamless and pictorial representations of topography, the earthy, chalky textures clearly distinguish and map the South Downs landscape. Uncannily familiar, rolling hills surrounded by the sea, more than the place itself, yet seemingly devoid of man-made structures.

The virtues of not-knowing…I think about Mockford's quote on the 'strangeness' of life and begin linking it to present day concepts of a complex, uncertain, and increasingly undemocratic world. How do you decide which path to take when life moves beyond the human scale? With AI expanding and taking over the fabric of everyday lives it's no wonder so many feel left behind with outdated knowledge and beliefs. Bombarded by a stream of information daily rituals involve attempting to operate barely understood systems and technology. Often it seems I am reduced to just pressing buttons for the sake of it. Contrast these concerns with the 'unknowingness' Mockford referred to, which seems more like a romantic adventure into the process of composition. Although he sometimes worked from memory, he usually carried a small sketchbook on walks and visits on the Downs. He recorded scenes in pencil and ink accompanied with scribbled notes of particular colours or topographical references. Many of these places were already etched into the personal habitat absorbed in his childhood. At that time playing out on the Downs would have offered protection too, away from the more industrial targets of enemy bombers. In Mockford's poetic celebration of the genius loci, there is no mention of depiction, observation, or recall. Everything is not what it seems. His paintings were only said to be complete when they reached that 'perfect moment of strangeness'.

Being and belonging. From the familiar to the unfamiliar, moving from memory into the dream mode…Mockford memorably referred to this process as 'recapturing the wonder' in a 2012 essay for The London Magazine by poet Peter Abbs. The scientific studies of physical characteristics in early abstracts like *Eastbourne* also provided a source of drama and narrative while recreating the intangible curves and shapes of the Downs. Undoubtedly, in 1958 not many locals would have recognised the exact location. Yet few could surely fail to note the mysterious and alluring undulation of chalk hills with paths excavated into the canvas, a sprinkling of sheep and the willowy church spire climbing through a clomp of trees. Standing proud, cut deep into the central hillside with a stave in each hand, the Long Man of Wilmington is the veritable elephant in the room. Whenever visiting my mother, I always attempt to prise her out of the stifling, cauldron bubble of the care home lounge. Day in, day out, she sits there with the wayward sisters causing comical mischief. Most of their time appears to be spent obsessing over food. Often the Beckettian ritual goes on and on until a member of staff appears round the door to announce the next meal. Escaping in the car for a few hours we drift through several of the locations that provided inspiration for Mockford's paintings. Passing a steady stream of faceless tourists skimming the uneven grassy verge leading to Birling Gap and the Belle Tout lighthouse, part of the world famous Seven Sisters. Hung like white curtains along the flat green coast, the iconic cliffs draw people from all over the world, year in, year out. Popular, but vulnerable to coastal erosion, the small rural clifftop could give way at any given moment.

With the post-Covid boom in visitor numbers rising to over 600,000 people a year, the National Trust owned site banned coaches parking or dropping-off in the area. Seaford Head Local Nature Reserve at the end of the Seven Sisters walk covers a wide area eastwards to the Cuckmere Valley and north to Exceat Bridge. Formed out of microscopic plankton shells that compressed into chalk after sinking to the seabed in the Cretaceous period (between 65 and 100 million years ago), the resulting dome eroded into the gleaming ridges of the South Downs. The huge block of chalk at Seaford Head presides over a long esplanade with another significant French Connection. A small Napoleonic war-era Martello Tower, no.74 of the original 103 defensive forts built across the British Empire in the 19th century. On visits to Seaford, we always link arms during our short strolls along the promenade where the tower is situated. Often watching the comings and goings of the Newhaven-Dieppe ferry service, we usually take a much needed breather at one of the wooden benches. Soaking up the sun and sampling scoops of nostalgic happiness from the Carnival Ice Cream van. Mockford's *Seaford Head* painted in 1964 is another early abstract and favourite of mine. In freeform groups of casually drawn organic shapes painted with muted palette, he applied a thick impasto evoking Dubuffet's brutal beauty, childlike and raw. The strangeness feels right. Although the painting doesn't set out to achieve any sense of illustrative perfection, it nonetheless maintains an air of mystery centred in the landscape of East Sussex.

Mockford consistently embellished his observations. Amid scenes of impending drama, he bled the excitement of an impending catastrophe or moment of otherworldly revelation to create narratives where nothing is more significant than anything else. Everything is infinitely precious. Moving away from the grey monotone captured in *Eastbourne's* tactile relief, paintings like *Belle Tout* and *Cars at Birling Gap* are bathed in swirling psychedelic mauves and pinks. As the new cultural forms and subcultures unfolded, these vibrant works establish a connection with the hallucinatory counterculture sentiments of the late 1960s.

The solitary figure is another distinctive motif throughout Mockford's work, often suggesting an unresolved moment or invitation. I've experienced dozens of these flashes myself, gazing out beyond the harbour's mouth at Newhaven, off into the distance like the monk in Friedrich's whispering Zeitgeist. Human counterparts to the vastness of the sea. Meeting the non-measurable dying symphonies in the abyss where there is nothing, no depth, no perspective, only a fearful truth bound up with a void of mythology and mysticism. In the stillness of the Channel, a turbulent dead zone nurtures our disembodied memories...

In 1996, Mockford moved to Newhaven, installing a studio in his garage. In predominantly sunny weather, he first glimpsed the harbour on a visit to his good friend, Myrta Fisher, a fellow painter. The bobbing hulls and sound of anchor chains moving to the rhythm of the tides proffered further opportunities for potential fictions. From the new lounge window he began to witness a series of new developments spring up. Almost immediately the ferry port became another key motif in his work, adding to a list containing things like level crossings, trains and road junctions. Abandoning the studio, he began to paint the view from his living room at various times of day, framing paintings with the curtains while incorporating reflections from the walls. That which can be imagined is what happens...

Painted just before he moved to Newhaven, 1994's *Waiting to Go* captures a moment of almost pure abstraction. Contained within a painting of two halves, blue fluffy clouds guide the returning ferry boat back from Dieppe toward Newhaven harbour. Behind, a rectangular shaped wall built up with thick layers of rustic-hued impasto, echoes the 'music and poetry' of Rothko's emotionally seared transcendence. In the bottom half, above lines of parked cars and clustered buildings, the wires of two telegraph poles sag under the weight from a gulp of swallows. Waiting to migrate, *en attendant d'y aller*....Adding to the sense of melodrama, three tiny figures observe the incoming ferry from a solitary wooden gate, a gateway to the churning sea. The canvas as sail, in the sounds, sights and smells of the Channel mixing the changing qualities of light imbued with the weighty issues affecting the world.

The day after visiting my mother I spent a quiet hour at the Towner submerged in the *Drawing the Unspeakable* exhibition. Towards the end of some 300 works, a series of pieces challenge the prevailing themes of seascape urbanism, boundaries, displacement and war. One of them features a group project by refugees mainly from Africa waiting in camps near Paris for an opportunity to cross the Channel. Prisoners in the politics of loss and conflict, many produced books made out of cardboard boxes containing pencil drawings of left behind homes.

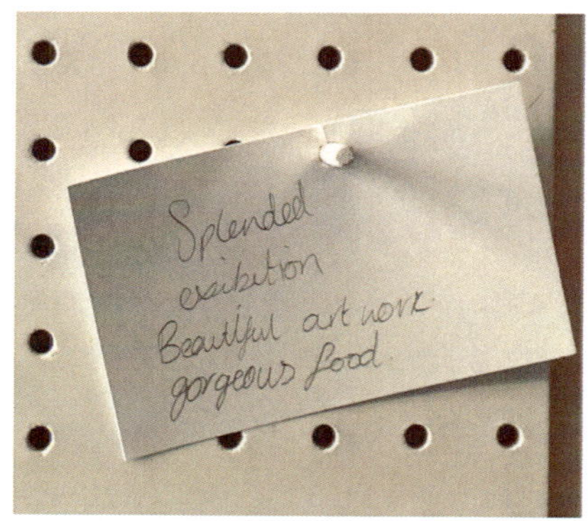

Ahmad's story is fragmented into scribbling on strips of cardboard...

"When I want to go in Europe, I am very scared. I don't know swimming.
La vie d'Ahmad a voyage...Life is jungle".

Points of Departure

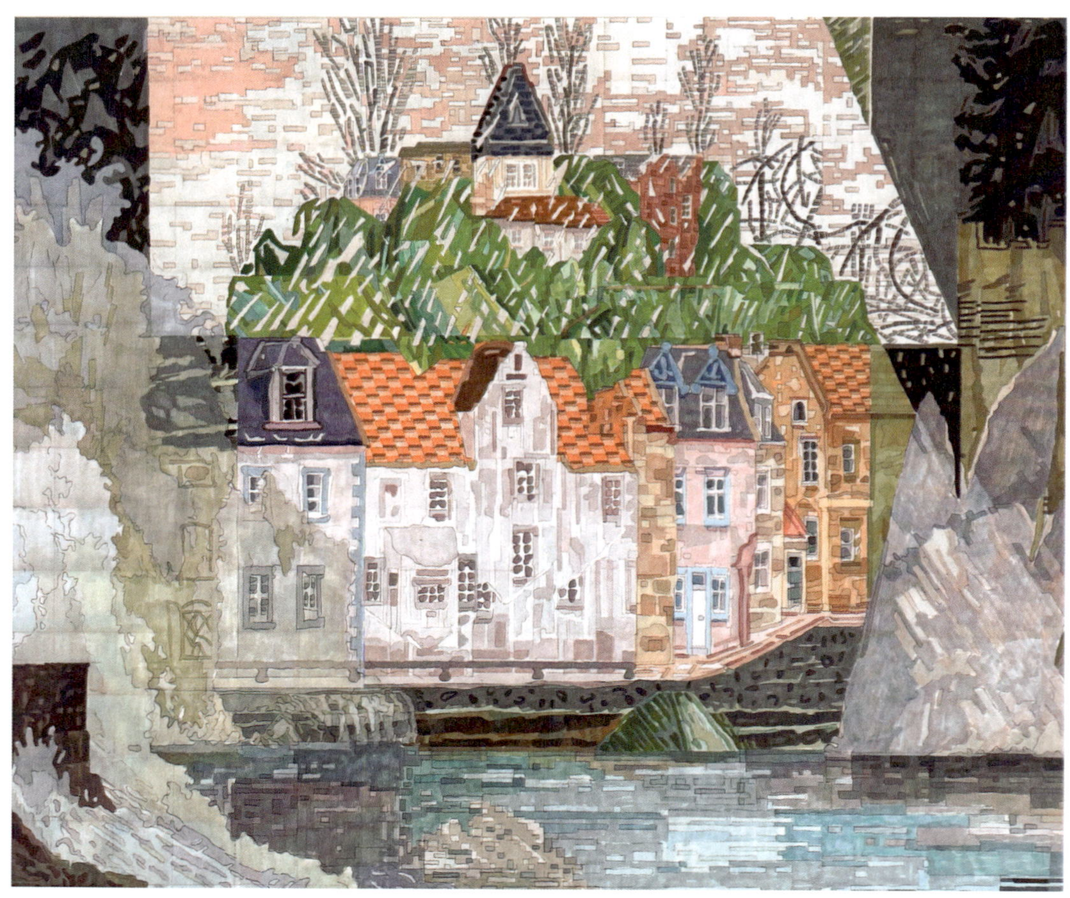

fig.7

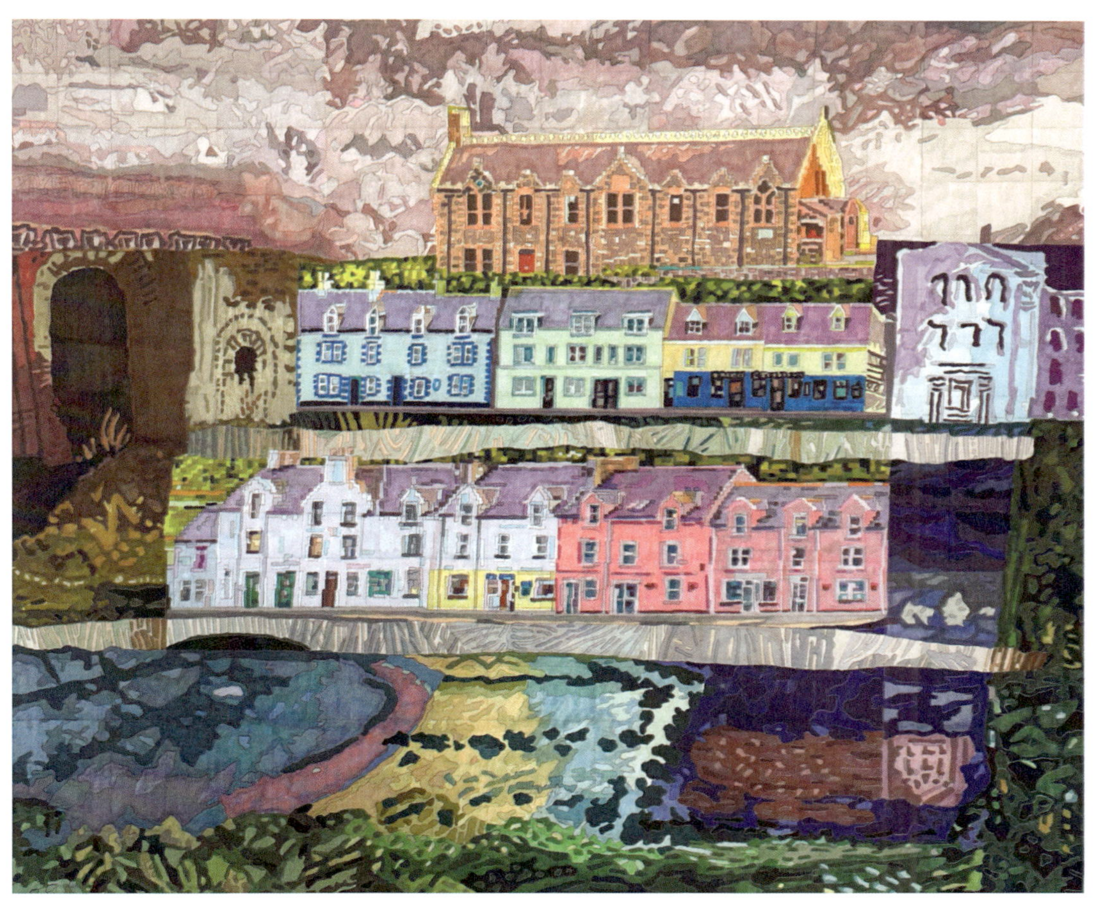

fig.8

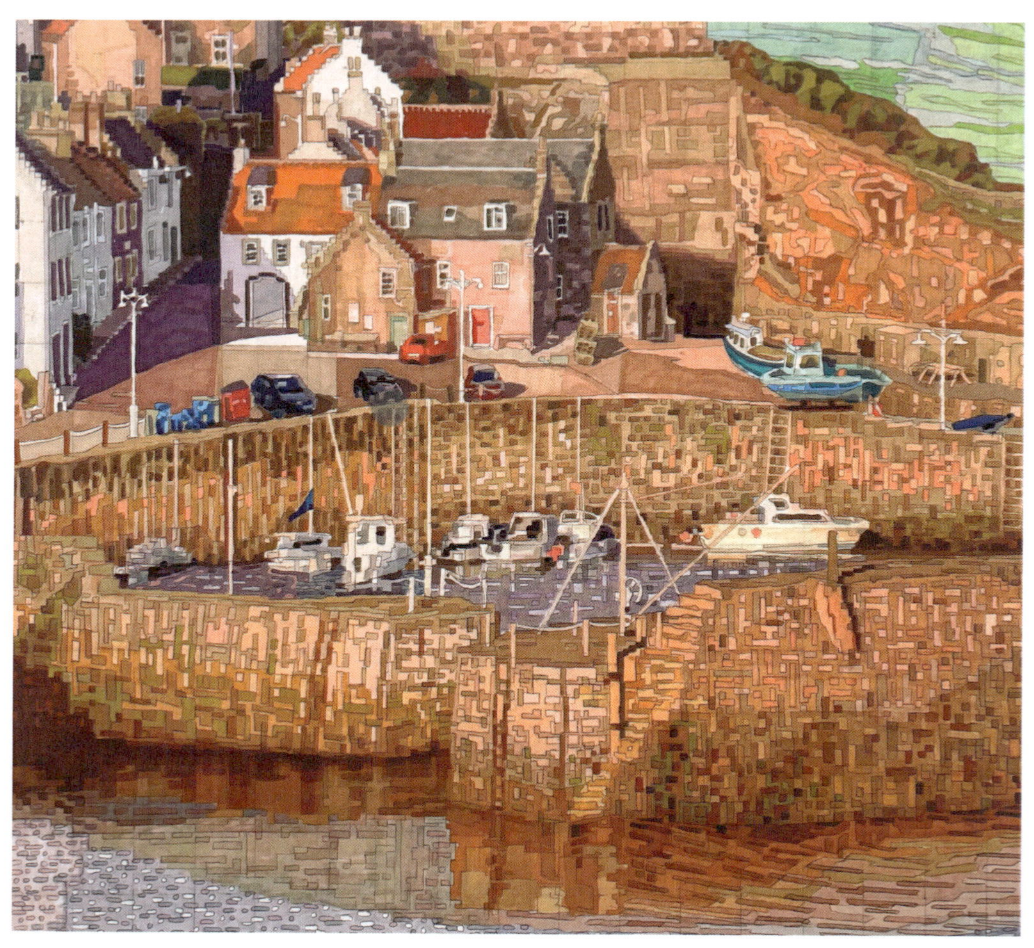

fig.9

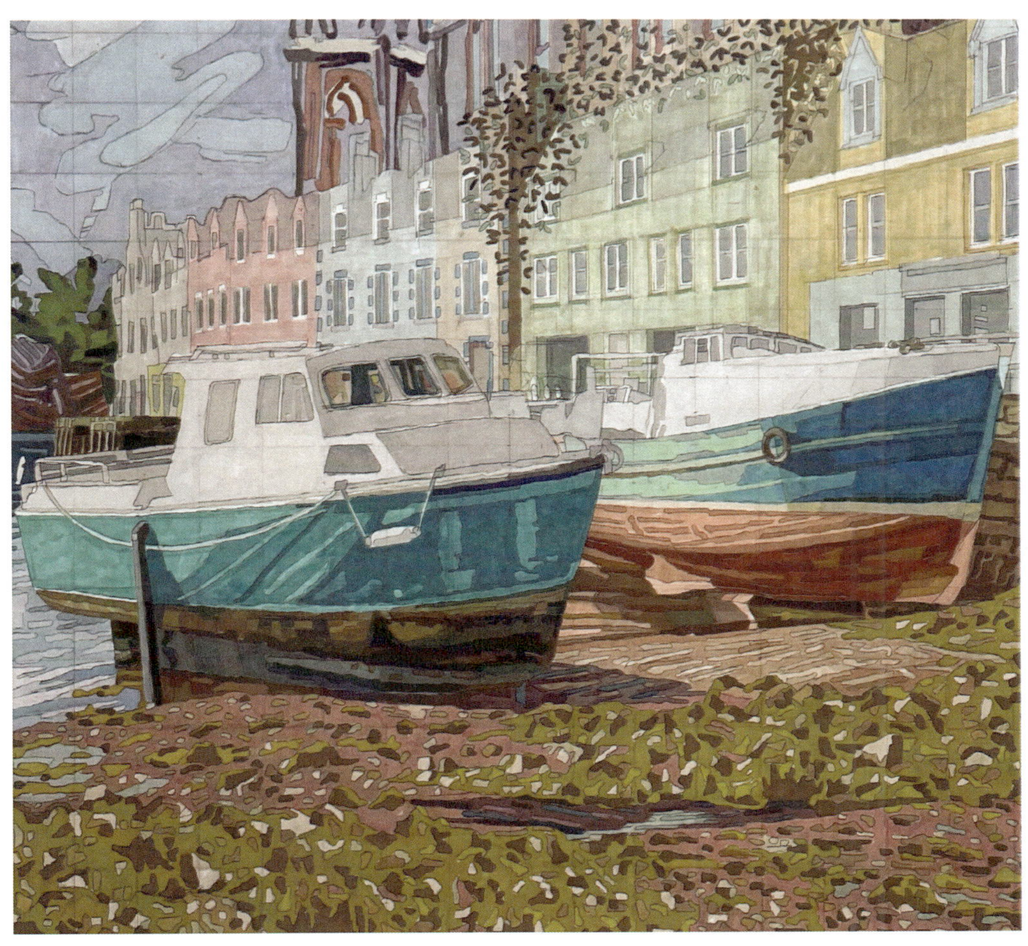

fig.10

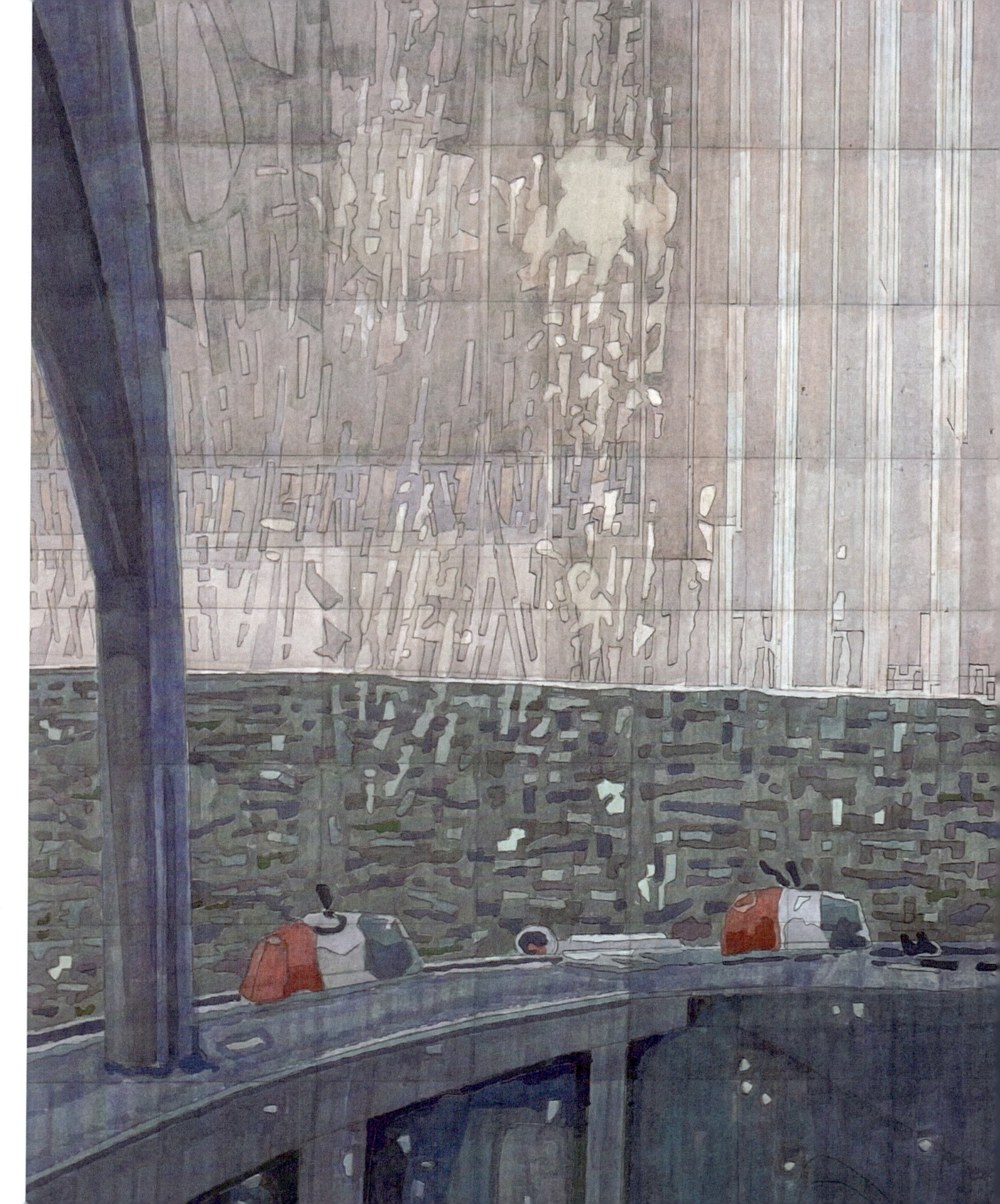

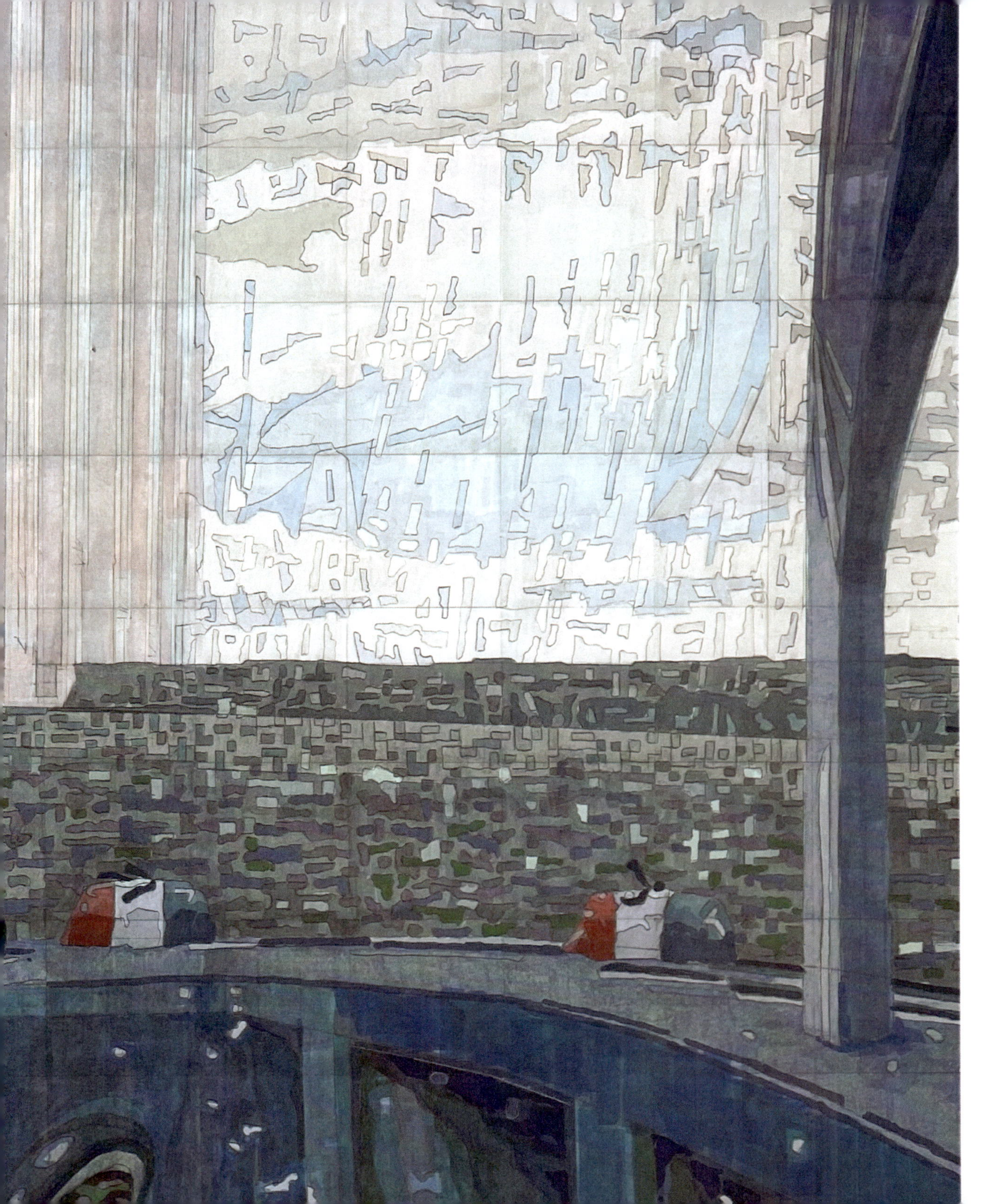

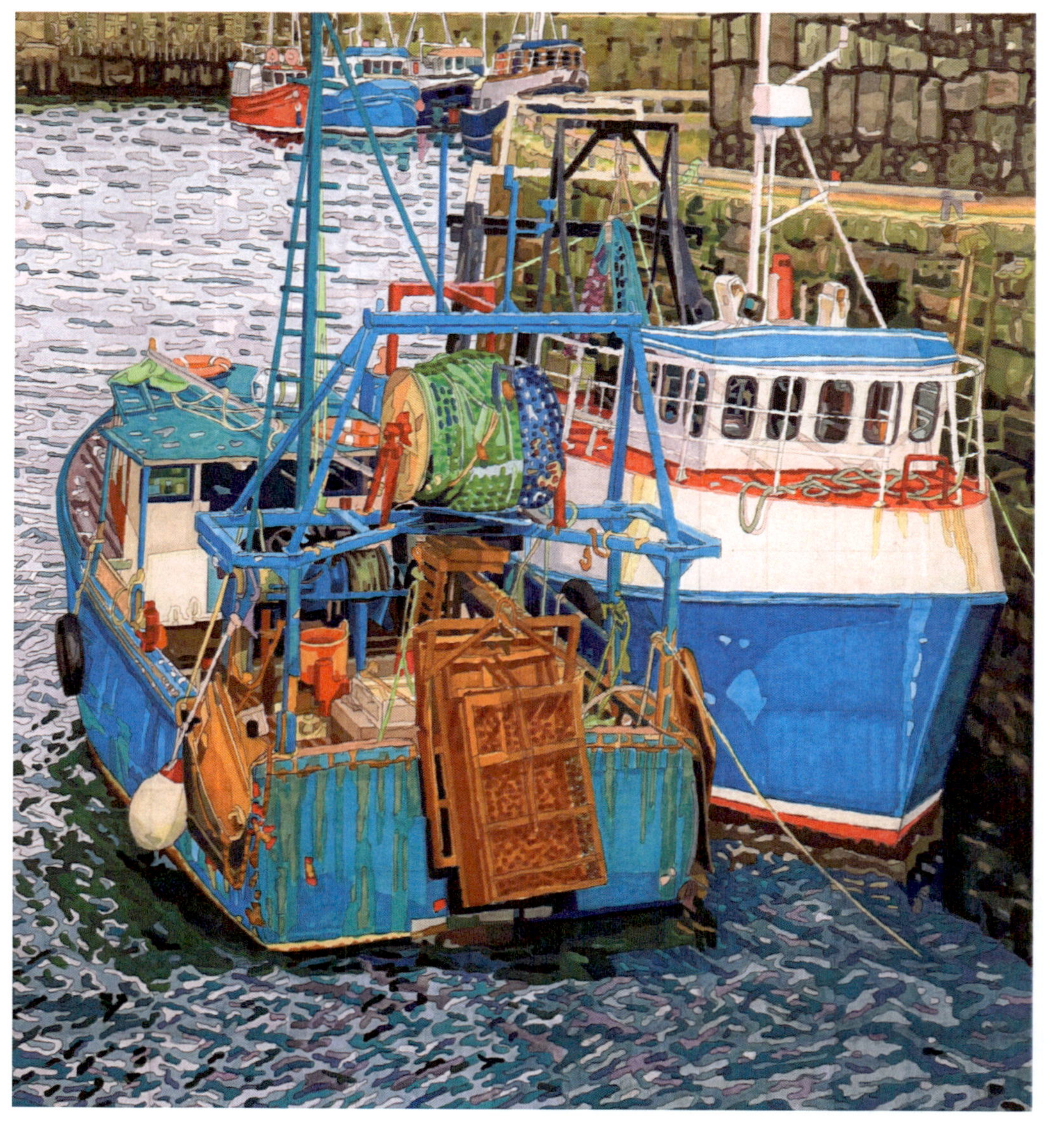

fig.12

fig.13

fig.1: *Dieppe Harbour,* pen and ink drawing, 2024 - Iain Sharpe
fig.2: *Harbour. I,* pen and ink drawing, 2023 - Iain Sharpe
fig.3: *Newhaven Harbour spoil tip,* photograph, 2022 - David Banning
fig.4: *La Manche,* pen and ink drawing, 2024 - Iain Sharpe
fig.5: *Harbour. IV,* pen and ink drawing, 2023 - Iain Sharpe
fig.6: *Britannia Beaver,* photograph, 2022 - David Banning
fig.7: *Sea Town in Storm,* pen and ink drawing, 2023 - Iain Sharpe
fig.8: *Sea Town after Storm,* pen and ink drawing, 2023 - Iain Sharpe
fig.9: *Harbour. III,* pen and ink drawing, 2023 - Iain Sharpe
fig.10: *Harbour. V,* pen and ink drawing, 2023 - Iain Sharpe
fig.11: *Côte d'Albâtre,* pen and ink drawing, 2024 - Iain Sharpe
fig.12: *Harbour. II,* pen and ink drawing, 2023 - Iain Sharpe
fig.13: *Sussex Bay,* photograph, 2023 - David Banning

Page 28 - Detail from Towner Art Gallery mural by Lothar Götz
Page 31 - Detail from *Eastbourne* by Harold Mockford
All other photographs/scribblings by David Banning

CHROMA EDITIONS

www.ingramcontent.com/pod-product-compliance
Lightning Source LLC
Chambersburg PA
CBRC091246050726
47599CB00010B/1004

9781838091576